22 DEC 2018

HAM

East Sussex
County Council

Please return or renew this item
by the last date shown. You may
return items to any East Sussex
Library. You may renew books
by telephone or the internet.

0345 60 80 195 for renewals
0345 60 80 196 for enquiries

Library and Information Services
eastsussex.gov.uk/libraries

04547639

info buzz

Islam

Izzi Howell

W

FRANKLIN WATTS

LONDON•SYDNEY

Franklin Watts
First published in Great Britain in 2018 by The Watts Publishing Group
Copyright © The Watts Publishing Group, 2018

Produced for Franklin Watts by
White-Thomson Publishing Ltd
www.wtpub.co.uk

All rights reserved

ISBN: 978 1 4451 5968 3
10 9 8 7 6 5 4 3 2 1

Credits
Series Editor: Izzi Howell
Series Designer: Rocket Design (East Anglia) Ltd
Designer: Clare Nicholas
Literacy Consultant: Kate Ruttle
Religious Consultant: Dr Suzanne Owen, Leeds Trinity University

The publisher would like to thank the following for permission to reproduce their pictures: Dreamstime: Muhammad Annurmal *cover*; Getty: Amanda Lewis 4, Mehmet Hilmi Barcin 6, Nikada 8, RobertHoetink 11b, Yuri_Arcurs 12l, Gideon Mendel/Corbis 13, Tubagus Aditya Irawan/Pacific Press/LightRocket 14, sauvik 18, Justin Merriman/Stringer 20; Shutterstock: Zurijeta *title page*, 11t and 17, szefei 5t, MaraZe 5b, Creativa Images 7, Aleks822 9, Jasminko Ibrakovic 10, Mrs_ya 12r, ZouZou 15, MidoSemsem 16, Gulsina 19t, arapix 19b, hikrcn 21l, AridOcean 21r.

Every attempt has been made to clear copyright. Should there be any inadvertent omission please apply to the publisher for rectification.

Printed in China

Franklin Watts
An imprint of
Hachette Children's Group
Part of The Watts Publishing Group
Carmelite House
50 Victoria Embankment
London EC4Y 0DZ

An Hachette UK Company
www.hachette.co.uk
www.franklinwatts.co.uk

All words in **bold** appear in the glossary on page 23.

Contents

What is Islam?

Islam is a religion. People who follow Islam are called Muslims. They pray to their God, Allah.

▲ Muslims worship at a mosque. They can also worship at home or at school.

Do you live near a mosque? Where is it?

4

Muslims follow rules. They should pray every day. They must give some of their money to poor people.

▲ This Muslim family is saving money in a jar to give to poor people.

◀ Muslims can eat chicken meat, but they don't eat **pork** (pig meat).

The Qur'an

Muslims believe that Allah spoke to a **prophet** called Muhammad. Allah told Muhammad how to be a Muslim. Allah's words are written down in a **holy** book, called the Qur'an.

▼ The Qur'an is written in a language called Arabic.

The Qur'an has stories about Allah. It has rules about how to be a good Muslim.

▼ This boy is learning to read the Qur'an with his father.

What do you read with your family?

The mosque

Muslims go to the mosque to pray, study and celebrate festivals.

Men and women pray in different parts of the mosque. ▼

The inside of a mosque is decorated with words from the Qur'an. There are no pictures or statues of people and animals.

words from the Qur'an

▲ This mosque has walls that are painted with words, shapes and flowers.

Praying

Some Muslims pray five times every day. In some places, someone sings from the mosque when it is time to pray.

▼ Muslims wash their hands, arms, face and feet before they pray.

When do you wash yourself?

Muslims **kneel** when they pray. They sit facing **Makkah**, the most holy Muslim city (see page 21).

▶ Muslims sometimes pray on soft mats.

▼ This arch shows the direction of Makkah for Muslims praying in the mosque.

arch

Clothes

Some Muslim women and girls wear special clothes. They cover their hair with a scarf called a **hijab**.

hijab

◀ These girls don't wear hijabs, but their mothers do.

▼ Some Muslim boys wear a special cap.

Some Muslim women don't wear a hijab. Other Muslim women choose to cover their face and body with **loose** clothes.

▲ It's easy to play while you are wearing a hijab.

A Muslim life

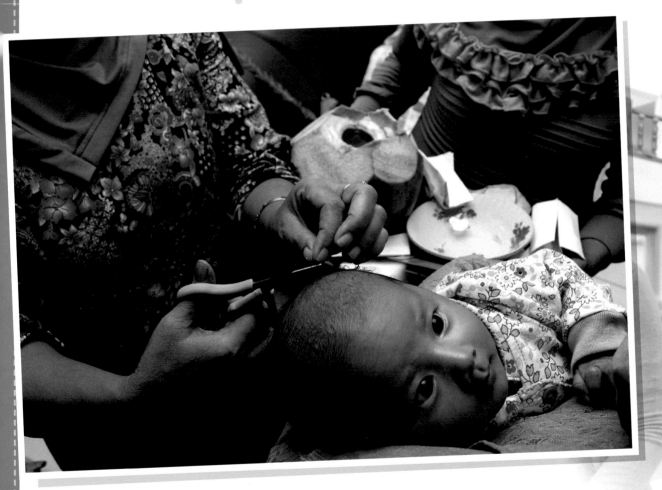

Muslims celebrate special moments during their life.

▲ Muslims have a celebration and cut a baby's hair when he or she is seven days old.

Muslims get married at the mosque. They make promises to look after each other.

What do you wear on a special day?

▼ Muslim brides often wear a white dress.

Ramadan

Ramadan is a Muslim festival that lasts for a month. Muslims try to pray more and read the Qur'an during Ramadan.

◄ **Some Muslims light colourful lanterns during Ramadan.**

Some Muslims **fast** during the day in Ramadan. They only eat before the sun comes up and after the sun goes down.

▼ Muslim families eat a special meal together after the sun goes down in Ramadan.

When do you eat a special meal with your family?

17

Id-ul-Fitr

Id-ul-Fitr is a festival that happens at the end of Ramadan. Muslims pray together. They also give each other presents and wear new clothes.

▲ On Id-ul-Fitr, some Muslims pray together in parks.

Muslims celebrate the end of Ramadan at Id-ul-Fitr. They eat a special meal during the daytime.

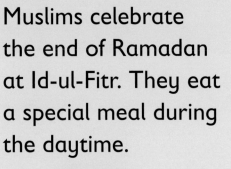

▲ Muslims often eat sweet pastries at Id-ul-Fitr.

◀ Some Muslim children eat biscuits to celebrate Id-ul-Fitr.

Around the world

Muslims live in many places around the world. There are Muslims in Africa, Europe, Asia and North America.

▼ These Muslims are celebrating Id-ul-Fitr in the United States of America (USA).

The holy city of Makkah is in the country of Saudi Arabia. Muslims must try to visit Makkah once in their life.

Makkah

▼ Many Muslims pray together in a special building in Makkah.

Quiz

Test how much you remember.

Check your answers on page 24.

1 Who is Allah?

2 Which parts of the body do Muslims wash before they pray?

3 What is a hijab?

4 When do some Muslims eat during Ramadan?

5 When is Id-ul-Fitr?

6 In which country is Makkah?

Glossary

fast – to not eat or drink for a certain time

hijab – a Muslim head scarf

holy – very important to a religion

kneel – to sit with one or two knees on the ground

lantern – a light that can be carried with a candle inside

loose – not tightly fitting

Makkah – the most holy Muslim city, found in the country of Saudi Arabia

pork – the meat from a pig

prophet – someone sent by God to tell people how to live

worship – to show that you think a god is important by praying or doing something religious

Index

Answers:

1: God for Muslims; 2: Hands, arms, face and feet; 3: A head scarf; 4: Before the sun comes up and after the sun goes down; 5: At the end of Ramadan; 6: Saudi Arabia

Teaching notes:

Children who are reading Bookband Gold or above should be able to enjoy this book with some independence. Other children will need more support. All children may benefit from help pronouncing unfamiliar words linked to Islam.

Before you share the book:

- Are any of the children in your class Muslim? Can they tell you about their experiences and understanding?
- Talk together about the beliefs of other children. What is the same/what is different from Muslim children's experiences?

While you share the book:

- Help children to read some of the more unfamiliar words and concepts.

- Talk about the questions. Encourage children of different faiths or no faith to share their own answers.
- Talk about the pictures. Help children to identify who or what the captions refer to. Talk about the Arabic writing that is read from right to left across the page (p7). Discuss the patterns on the walls of the mosque (p9).

After you have shared the book:

- Find out more about stories from the Qur'an. Are there any stories that are similar to stories of other religions?
- Arrange to take the children to visit a mosque. Ask them to look for things mentioned or shown in the book.
- Work through the free activity sheets from our Teacher Zone at www.hachettechildrens.co.uk

Series Contents Lists

Religion

978 1 4451 5962 1

What is Christianity?
The Bible
Going to church
Communion
Praying
A Christian life
Christmas
Easter
Around the world

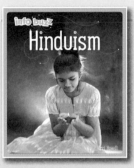

978 1 4451 5964 5

What is Hinduism?
Hindu books
The mandir
Worship
At home
A Hindu life
Divali
Holi
Around the world

978 1 4451 5968 3

What is Islam?
The Qur'an
The mosque
Praying
Clothes
A Muslim life
Ramadan
Eid al Fitr
Around the world

978 1 4451 5966 9

What is Judaism?
The Torah
The synagogue
Worship
Shabbat
A Jewish life
Hanukkah
Purim
Around the world

History

978 1 4451 5948 5

978 1 4451 5886 0

978 1 4451 5950 8

978 1 4451 5952 2

Countries

Argentina 978 1 4451 5958 4
India 978 1 4451 5960 7
Japan 978 1 4451 5956 0
The United Kingdom 978 1 4451 5954 6

FRANKLIN WATTS